IN THE
NATIONAL INTEREST

General Sir John Monash once exhorted a graduating class to 'equip yourself for life, not solely for your own benefit but for the benefit of the whole community'. At the university established in his name, we repeat this statement to our own graduating classes, to acknowledge how important it is that common or public good flows from education.

Universities spread and build on the knowledge they acquire through scholarship in many ways, well beyond the transmission of this learning through education. It is a necessary part of a university's role to debate its findings, not only with other researchers and scholars, but also with the broader community in which it resides.

Publishing for the benefit of society is an important part of a university's commitment to free intellectual inquiry. A university provides civil space for such inquiry by its scholars, as well as for investigations by public intellectuals and expert practitioners.

This series, In the National Interest, embodies Monash University's mission to extend knowledge and encourage informed debate about matters of great significance to Australia's future.

Professor Susan Elliott AM
Interim President and Vice-Chancellor,
Monash University

THE CONSULTANCY CONUNDRUM: THE HOLLOWING OUT OF THE PUBLIC SECTOR

EDITED BY LACHLAN GUSELLI & ANDREW JASPAN

MONASH
UNIVERSITY
PUBLISHING

Monash University Publishing
Matheson Library Annexe
40 Exhibition Walk
Monash University
Clayton, Victoria 3800, Australia
https://publishing.monash.edu

Monash University Publishing brings to the world publications which
advance the best traditions of humane and enlightened thought.

ISBN: 9781922979322 (paperback)
ISBN: 9781922979346 (ebook)

Series: In the National Interest
Editor: Greg Bain
Project manager & copyeditor: Paul Smitz
Designer: Peter Long
Typesetter: Cannon Typesetting
Proofreader: Gillian Armitage
Printed in Australia by Ligare Book Printers

A catalogue record for this book is available from the National Library of
Australia.

THE CONSULTANCY CONUNDRUM: THE HOLLOWING OUT OF THE PUBLIC SECTOR

INTRODUCTION

Lachlan Guselli, Sydney Commissioning Editor for 360info; and Andrew Jaspan, Editor-in-Chief of 360info

On the eve of Australia's last federal election in 2022, then-prime minister Scott Morrison announced that his Liberal–National Coalition government, if re-elected, would cut $3.3 billion from the Australian Public Service (APS). Over the next four years, 5500 jobs would be slashed from the APS to pay for the potential new government's election promises. Morrison claimed the multibillion-dollar cut 'doesn't impact on programs or services at all'. A year later, following a public service audit, it was revealed Morrison's government spent $20.8 billion outsourcing work in 2021–22. *The Guardian* reported that, during that time, 54 000 full-time staff were employed as consultants—the equivalent of 37 per cent of the public service.

Cuts to the APS are nothing new. This act, in context, matches the overwhelming narrative of Western governance since the 1980s and its co-existence with the neoliberal doctrine. Neoliberalism as an economic theory has always been hard to define, which could be why the International Monetary Fund took until 2016 to admit its existence explicitly. It is, however, considered to be at its core the 'liberalising of global markets associated with the reduction of state power'.[1] As Dr Marty Bortz asserts in his essay in this book, from Canberra to London, the 'underlying logic was that the private sector knows best. Private-sector management techniques were hypothetically introduced to produce better public-sector outcomes. Whether new public management has done this or not remains a heated point of debate.'

The cuts seen in Australia are reflected in civil service departments across the developed world, from the United Kingdom to the United States and Canada. To begin with, the ideology was a heady mixture of the spoils of the Cold War era of Reagan and Thatcher, including their commitment to deregulation, and a reimagined social contract between the government and its people. Ronald Reagan claimed in his inaugural address as US president: 'In this present crisis, government is not the solution to our problem; government is the problem.'

This period, which led to previously unthinkable wealth, had a counterweight. Much of the work to control the extremities of capitalism and industry is done by

governments. However, they had now either been sup-
pressed or removed altogether, or they had wilfully joined
the parade of deregulation.

In Australia, these cuts cannot be blamed on one side of
politics. Caps to the APS from 2015 pinned the workforce
back to the same employment numbers—167 596—as in
2006. Consecutive governments led by both major parties
have employed the policy of the efficiency dividend since
1986, which creates an annual reduction in resources. And
the breaking up of agencies is seen back in another age,
first with Labor hero Gough Whitlam in the 1970s, then
in earnest under the conservative government of Malcolm
Fraser. Fraser's government was accused of 'lobotomising
the public service' after it eliminated various agencies and
put ceilings on bureaucrat numbers.[2]

While the relationship between the government
and its civil service may have changed since the 1980s,
the latter's responsibilities have continued. External
consultants have filled the fundamental roles of service
delivery and providing frank and fearless advice in
some capacities. Andrew Podger writes in his essay that
'Ideology began to play a more explicit part from the late
1990s in Australia', describing a '*Yellow Pages* approach
… where any activities that private businesses revealed
in the *Yellow Pages* that they delivered were not to be
undertaken by government itself but instead outsourced'.
Indeed, 'privatised policymaking' became a growing
concern as governments further relied on these agencies

for digital transformation and advisory services into the twenty-first century. Podger reflects that 'the scale of increased political control and use of external labour over the last three decades has adversely affected the capability and performance of the APS'.

The so-called 'Big Four' consultancies, being PricewaterhouseCoopers (PwC), Ernst & Young (EY), Deloitte and KPMG, did well out of the trade winds of this age. In 2021, the global consulting services market was valued at between US$700 billion and US$900 billion. However, the COVID-19 pandemic changed how many perceive government services and the civil servants who deliver these programs. Consultancy firms were contracted to perform government work in massive numbers, but the concept that the private sector knows best ran parallel to the public narrative of nurses, doctors and other government employees being cheered in the streets.

In the United Kingdom, which early on had one of the highest COVID death rates, government work increasingly was being given to the major consulting firms without competition for contracts or oversight of value for money. By 2022, the National Health Service (NHS) had quadrupled its budget for outside advice as the UK Government contracted out £2.8 billion worth of work to consultants alone. As a consequence, when the government required the state to perform its functions during a crisis, it was left under-resourced and stretched to capacity.

Across the developed world, the major consulting firms dominated during COVID-19. According to an industry website, 'PwC and Accenture in Australia join a global body of leading consulting firms working on vaccine delivery strategies ... While Accenture, Boston Consulting Group, Deloitte, PwC, and McKinsey are all among the lead consultants of the UK's vaccination programme.'[3] Denis Saint-Martin and Chris Hurl claim in their essay that, because of the pandemic, privatised policymaking suddenly became more visible to the public: 'In many countries, the high costs of using consultants became politically noisy, with governments and consulting firms feeling the backlash.'

So, while Morrison's attempted cuts to the APS were nothing new, they were promised to a changed electorate that held a fresh set of expectations of the state. What the Morrison government was offering, six months after the end of major east-coast COVID lockdowns that saw Sydney and Melbourne segregated, was to channel money away from the government's ability to develop, implement and manage programs to support communities. Instead, the money apparently was going to be better spent on BMX tracks and dog parks in marginal electorates.

After Anthony Albanese's Labor Party won the 2022 election, the new Minister for the Public Service, Katy Gallagher, said the former government promoted a 'mirage of efficiency but were at the same time spending almost $21bn of public money on a shadow workforce that was deliberately kept secret'. To fulfil the promises the government could not deliver due to public service cuts, it did what it has always done in this position in recent years, regardless of which party is in power: called on external consultants and contractors to do the job.

In handing over government to the Albanese administration, the Coalition failed the test set by a former Liberal prime minister. John Howard told a room of public servants in 1997 at the Garran Oration, less than a year after sacking multiple department secretaries and high-level functionaries, that 'the responsibility of any government must be to pass on to its successors a public service which is better able to meet the challenges of its time than the one it inherited'.

One media report said the scale of institutional memory lost to the APS in 2022 'means that one of the country's core institutions suffers a form of organisational dementia'.[4] The current government inherited an APS that had been slowly perishing for decades, with an estimated 13 000 to 18 000 jobs cut since the Coalition under Tony Abbott took power in 2013. In a Faustian bargain, the public service has become what one academic calls a 'captive of the industry': with less investment in services, the government has been spending more on consultants to fill public service gaps, who then advise that more consultants should be brought in.[5]

By the very nature of their establishment, external contractors are accountable to their employers first, not their employers' contracts. Christopher Wright points out in his essay that 'their survival depends upon winning and maintaining client relationships such that an ongoing line of business contracts is maintained'.

According to The Australia Institute, less than 20 per cent of consultants' reports to the government are published, a failing that implies governments could seek advice from consultants in line with the answers they want, as opposed to the reality of a situation. Governments can then blame consultants for news the public may not wish to receive. However, say Denis Saint-Martin and Chris Hurl, governments are not just unfortunate witnesses to unscrupulous consultancy firms, but 'influence the decision to hire outside experts by creating uncertainty while also offering a readily available solution. They make clients addicted to, or over-reliant on, their expertise.'

A significant concern surrounding the increased work of consultants is accountability. The APS is held to account and must act in the public interest under codes of conduct bound by government Acts. But as Stuart Kells writes in this book, 'as well as standing alongside public-sector clients as trusted advisers, the Big Four sometimes sit on the opposite side of the table, advising corporates and other entities in conflict with government and, sometimes, in conflict with the public interest'.

The Centre for Public Integrity has released data showing that the Big Four in Australia saw a 1270 per cent increase in their work from 2012 to 2022. At the same time, they also contributed over $4 million in donations to the two major political parties. This arrangement came into sharp public focus in 2023 when the Australian affiliate of PwC was accused of misusing confidential government tax information for commercial gain. PwC had been tasked with advising the federal government on the design of stricter multinational tax laws and had been leaking that same information to help other clients evade potential new taxes.

Despite the unfolding saga, PwC still holds significant consultancy contracts with the Australian Government worth an estimated $500 million. Andrew Podger believes that having long-term contractors sit beside APS employees doing similar ongoing work raises a fundamental constitutional issue, as questions of accountability and the potential subversion of executive power fail to be adequately addressed. 'If they [the consultants] are in effect Commonwealth employees, they should be employed under powers authorised by the parliament such, as the *Public Service Act*. That might also make them subject to legislated codes of conduct,' he writes here. Consultants are currently not held to those requirements.

The PwC tax scandal in isolation is shocking. But the involvement of PwC in the Robodebt debacle speaks to a pattern. PwC was employed to undertake 'an independent review of the compliance and fraud activities' within the Department of Human Services, with the expectation of a 100-page report. What was delivered was an eight-slide

PowerPoint presentation. For that, the firm received $853 859. PwC would return the cash after its involvement in these twin scandals became public knowledge, but the money is a mere drop in the ocean for these global behemoths.

The task of unpicking the influence of these consultancies, and addressing concerns over ethics and conflicts of interest, continues to occupy governments across the world, including Australia's. Calls for increased regulation and greater transparency are just the beginning of this debate, with James Guthrie and Allan Fels suggesting in their essay that the time has come to thoroughly scrutinise how the Big Four operate: 'As a matter of priority, the various parliamentary inquiries now underway should investigate conflicts of interest and dubious ethical practices by the Big Four and those legal firms that provide aggressive taxation advice.'

The world is watching on as these firms are dragged before Senate and committee hearings in Australia, in an effort to discover how deep the rot goes in our civil service.[6]

THE SHADOW GOVERNMENT PLUNDERING THE PUBLIC PURSE

Marty Bortz, University of Melbourne

The controversy surrounding PwC has many asking whether the hundreds of millions of dollars government departments spend on consultants each year is the best use of public money. PwC is under intense scrutiny after it was alleged the firm misused confidential government tax information for commercial gain. It is alleged that, after the firm advised the government on tougher tax laws, it then leaked the design of those laws to its clients—many of whom would be targeted by the proposed laws.

This is not the first time this issue has been investigated. Three recent examples are the 2019 Thodey review of the APS, a 2017 Australian National Audit Office (ANAO) audit of Commonwealth departments' use of consultants and contractors, and a 2014 audit by the Victorian Auditor-General's Office (VAGO). You could be forgiven for dismissing this matter as an insider issue of public administration best left to the boffins to thrash out. However, as the PwC scandal illustrates, the excessive use of consultants has very real implications for democratic decision-making. Indeed, many experts argue the influx of consultants represents a shadow government that is plundering the public sector. Some go so far as to say that it represents private control over public policy. It is therefore timely to consider why governments use consultants so much, why that might be a problem, and what we can do about it.

The consulting industry can be traced back to the father of so-called 'scientific management', Frederick Winslow Taylor, and his cohort of 'efficiency engineers', which included such business luminaries as Henry Gantt, Lillian and Frank Gilbreth, and Harrington Emerson. This group could be considered the first management consultants. They were involved in advising the US Government on matters of efficiency, administration and organisational design; for example, the Hoover Commission in 1947 hired two consulting firms to provide advice on reforms to public administration. Likewise, political scientist Denis Saint-Martin has described the 1960 Canadian Glassco Commission on Government Reorganisation as 'by far the most impressive demonstration of the influence of consultants in government'.

Consultants received a massive shot in the arm through the introduction of a bundle of reforms collectively known as the new public management. This introduced into government hands-on professional public management, explicit performance measures, an emphasis on 'output controls', competition in the public sector, and the disaggregation of units in the public sector. It also stressed private-sector styles of management practice.

After the advent of new public management, spending on consultants rose dramatically. In the United Kingdom, spending on consultants by the Department of Defence from 1993 to 2006 increased from £55 million to £256 million. Over the same period, spending by the Home Office increased from £3.81 million to £125 million—a change of 3190 per cent.

New public management arrived in the 1980s when the economic ideas of UK prime minister Margaret Thatcher and US president Ronald Reagan held sway. It represented a victory of private-sector ideology over the public. The underlying logic was that the private sector knows best. Private-sector management techniques were hypothetically introduced to produce better public-sector outcomes. Whether new public management has done this or not remains a heated point of debate. At the very least, it has created an environment in which consultants can thrive.

It has also been a major contributor to the loss of expertise in government. As political science Professor Rod Rhodes described it many years ago, the state has been 'hollowed out'.[7] With governments turning to consultants more and more, public servants have not been doing the necessary work to upgrade their skills and increase their expertise. The consultants have been gaining that expertise and—for a fee—providing their advice to bureaucrats. Reliance on consultants has become more entrenched, and now we are in a situation where they are seen as a 'shadow' public service.

The presence of consultants on its own is not a problem. Decision-makers throughout the ages have turned to advisers to assist with pressing challenges. Besides, the nature of governing today is far more complex than it was even a few decades ago. It is prudent, therefore, to turn to a range of different sources for advice—including consultants. And there are situations where very highly specialised or technical knowledge is required to support public decision-making. However, while the principle of consultants being part of governing today is sound, the practice is a problem. There are four parts to this problem: definition, quantity, management and procurement.

The problem of definition relates to the public sector's understanding of what consultants are and what they do. There is confusion as to how consultants differ from contractors and, as a result, how best to deploy them. This issue is fundamental to the nature of work that consultants are asked to do and how governments report on the extent of consultancy spending. It means work more appropriately classified as a contractor's can be attributed to a consultancy, and vice versa. It also means departments can pay a premium for the services of a consultant when a (much cheaper) contractor would suffice. It also might result in contractors putting up substandard work, thereby damaging the reputation of consultants generally.

The problem of quantity relates to how often governments use consultants. VAGO recently estimated that the current Victorian Labor government on average has spent $140 million on consultants each year over the past five years. If we assume that the average cost of a consulting project is $100 000, then that's 1400 consulting projects across the state government—roughly 140 per department per year. While large, this pales in comparison to the United Kingdom's spend: £2.8 billion worth of consulting work in 2022 alone.

This issue of quantity is not just about 'how much'. It is also about 'who'. The bulk of consulting work is often awarded to the Big Four: KPMG, Deloitte, PwC and EY. The sheer volume of work, compounded by the awarding of work to a select group of firms, suggests governments are dependent on these specific firms. One UK official even warned others about getting 'addicted to having well trained, hard working people running around'.

The management problem relates to poor supervision of consultants. Department officials sometimes see consulting work as 'set and forget', meaning they don't actively manage or take ownership of the process or the results. This may result in something that is not fit for purpose, and so additional spending might be necessary to rectify a report or unwanted outcome. Consultants can often be put in a position of power over their clients where the client does not necessarily understand the work the consultant is doing. Ideally, a consulting project should be co-owned by the bureaucrat and the consultant.

The issue here is that bureaucrats end up defaulting to a consultant when internal staff might be more than capable of doing the work. In addition, the insecurity of public-sector work can sometimes mean consultants themselves become the keepers of institutional memory. If the right structures aren't put in place, this can further erode the expertise of the public sector, and the presence of consultants is made more necessary.

Finally, there is the problem of procurement. The traditional model assumes consulting services can be purchased just like any other good. However, the reality of purchasing consulting services is very different from, say, purchasing a piece of infrastructure. Consultants are often in relationships of co-dependency with government officials that transcend individual transactions. And the way in which procurement is practised often disguises these relationships, thus creating challenges in holding consultants accountable. Accountability issues are further compounded given that consultants can hide behind commercial-in-confidence privileges.

To address these issues, we first need to rebuild the policy capacity of the public service. Consultants should only be called in when a task requires a highly specialised form of knowledge combined with a deep understanding of, and relationships with, the specific sector. In the short term, consultants could be required to upskill the public service in its processes and methodologies. As my own research has demonstrated, this does happen, though it might not be common practice.[8]

Internal consulting divisions within the government are a possibility. Interestingly, Australia's current Labor government has committed to doing just that at the same time as the UK Cabinet Office is shutting its own down due to a lack of effectiveness. But the real piece of work is long-term generational change. A career path for public servants and considering policy work a genuine profession can help. This could involve better links between the public service and universities. It could see public departments define workforce needs and talk directly to universities about how those needs can be filled. It could consider public policy knowledge a genuine form of professional knowledge in its own right—similar to law or accounting.

This is going to take several years to get right, largely because Australia is now trying to wind back several decades of neoliberal ideology—not something that can be done overnight. Public servants could be trained in the best ways to work with consultants. On the flip side, consultants who want to work in government services could be required to undertake a professional accreditation that demonstrates they understand the important contextual differences between the public and private sectors.

In addition, procurement rules could be updated to remove the category of 'consulting' altogether. It causes too much confusion. Rather, categories could be based on the type of expertise that is actually being purchased. For instance, governments often purchase evaluation services, but 'evaluation' is not a recognised category in AusTender. Likewise, strategy advice and analytics are commonly provided consulting services but are typically subsumed under the much broader category of 'management and business professionals and administrative services'. These high-level categories can obscure as much as they reveal.

The approach to procurement and the associated rules applicable to consultants could also be overhauled to recognise the fundamentally relational—not transactional—ways in which consultants enter the public sector. Forms of 'relational contracting' could be investigated to allow for more transparency in the ways consultants are used. Consultancies could be subject to a set of ethical rules and professional standards.

Consulting doesn't 'look like' any other profession. There is no academic qualification, no professional standards and no regulatory body. In short, anybody can set up shop and call themselves a consultant. Addressing this issue would go a long way towards ensuring money is spent appropriately and provides quality outcomes to government.

There is a role for consultants to play in modern systems of government. At the same time, a lot needs to be done to ensure that we rein in the excessive public expenditure on private forms of advice. While there are several ideas that could be implemented in the short term, the real fix is to move away from ideologically privileging the private sector to recognising the unique value that public policy analysis and public servants can provide.

This isn't just a structural reform but a shift in perspective and culture. We can't unscramble the omelette, but we can certainly make it taste better.

Dr Marty Bortz is an Honorary Senior Fellow at the Melbourne School of Government at the University of Melbourne. He has worked in local and state government, and private consulting, across multiple portfolios.

CONSULTANTS AND THE BEAST WITH
SEVEN HEADS

Stuart Kells, La Trobe University

The world's biggest consulting firms have grown large and profitable by walking both sides of the street in their relationships with governments. The Big Four—PwC, Deloitte, EY and KPMG—have branched out from accountancy and auditing into new areas, and as they have done so, their own dangers and exposures have multiplied. Each new service line has brought with it a bundle of new risks. At the same time, the diversification of the major accounting firms has presented new risks for governments, which have been influenced by the misplaced idea that the firms are systemically important and therefore too big to fail.

There were warnings five years ago that the cultural and commercial tensions facing the Big Four would necessitate radical changes in how they are structured and how they operate. Today, those tensions have predictably intensified, and the firms' diversification strategy is no longer viable. In Australia, the PwC scandal has enabled a rare level of scrutiny and criticism. It is not an exaggeration to say that the firms are fighting to preserve their social licence to operate.

The reason why is simple: their failure to manage the conflicting interests of diversified firms. A PwC tax partner, who was privy to secret information about

Commonwealth Government plans to address tax avoidance, shared this information with some other PwC partners, and they reportedly used it to market tax-minimisation services to major commercial clients. The allegations are now at the centre of a Senate inquiry into the four firms and how they operate.

Through an organic process of mergers and expansion over more than 100 years, the Big Four have come to dominate public company auditing around the world. And through the firms' parallel 'supermarket' strategy of diversification, they now offer services that span a diverse range of fields including management consulting, corporate finance, tax, infrastructure, insolvency, marketing, information technology (IT), human resources and the law. Until recently, the strategy of diversification and growth served the firms well. They built strong positions in several other markets beyond traditional accounting and auditing, including the provision of advice and other services to governments. Now employing nearly 1.5 million staff and collecting US$190 billion in annual revenue, the firms have travelled a long way from their modest origins in the provision of a narrow set of accounting and audit services.

In 2018, KPMG's Australian chair Alison Kitchen remarked that her firm had enjoyed almost double-digit growth for the five years up to that point, adding: 'With the economy growing at about 3 per cent during that time, clearly that cannot continue indefinitely or else we'd end up taking over the world.' From the point of view of governments, the Big Four collectively are a seven-headed beast.

To begin with—the first head of the beast—governments care about corporate conduct and the integrity of financial information. Accordingly, governments care about, and are eager consumers of, the public good outcomes that arise from corporate audits. Those outcomes are aligned with, and supportive of, the goals that governments seek through corporate regulation. The activities of the Big Four also align with the goals of government in other ways. They have long served as sources of, and training grounds for, junior staff looking to work in public-sector roles that entail accounting and audit skills and nearby capabilities.

Second, around the world, governments are prominent direct purchasers of Big Four products and services, such as evaluations, business cases, forensic investigations, policy reviews, stakeholder engagement support, market soundings, internal audits, asset valuations and project-management services. The Big Four also serve as a 'body shop' or resource bank for governments, by enabling the temporary or permanent outsourcing of public-sector functions. Government purchases of Big Four services extend across a wide range of major portfolios, including defence, health care, infrastructure and utilities, education, research bodies and environmental management. They also extend across all levels of government, including the local level.

Within Western governments, Big Four advisory reports serve a complex anthropological purpose. When ministers and senior officials are making decisions about the use of public money and state power, the presence of a Big Four–branded report is often a source of safety and reassurance. Until recently in Australia, few people were ever fired for engaging a Big Four consultant to provide advice.

Sometimes, the perceived value of a Big Four advisory report is warranted, but more than once, such reports have functioned merely to wrap a non-government veneer or security blanket around something that officials already knew, and could have produced themselves (see the fourth head of the beast, below). Sometimes, the reports are long and deliver a satisfying 'thud', even though the analysis and findings could have been expressed more succinctly. (This 'thud factor' is sometimes a basis for the pricing of consulting reports.) And sometimes, the reports are merely examples of what organisational behaviour expert André Spicer has aptly termed 'business bullshit'.

In these and other ways, Big Four products serve complex functions in how politicians, officials and government agencies fulfil their own roles and manage their own risks. The anthropological value of Big Four reports is highly vulnerable to episodes such as tax scandals and botched audits that damage the Big Four brands.

Third, as organisations, the Big Four operate conspicuously outside the frameworks for taxation and corporate governance that apply to corporations. This is because they are not corporations at all. They are owned by their partners, rather than shareholders, and they are not subject to typical corporate reporting and auditing requirements. But aspects of the Big Four's activities do attract the attention of the regulatory and oversight functions of governments. In the United States, for example, the Public Company Accounting Oversight Board oversees the quality of Big Four assurance services.

In Australia, some Big Four tax services are scrutinised (with mixed success) by bodies such as the Tax Practitioners Board (TPB) and the Australian Taxation Office (ATO), but the PwC leaks scandal has led to a multipronged regulatory response. Australia's federal Treasurer Jim Chalmers has promised to strengthen the TPB, for example, and other responses are emerging in the domains of competition policy, integrity agencies, law enforcement and the courts. Although the Big Four are not subject to external audits in the way public corporations are, aspects of their activities could be subject to more audit-style scrutiny.

One example is the pending demerger of PwC's government advisory business into the new entity Scyne Advisory in Australia. The new entity is a corporation, with outside shareholders. The carve-out of this business gives rise to numerous practical problems, and potentially more serious legal and contractual ones, such as with regard to existing government engagements, membership of government 'panels', and the handling of government client files. For instance, if a government client has contracted with PwC, and PwC is now withdrawing from that service area, and Scyne intends to take over that service area, can Scyne have access to historical files and other information?

Carving out Scyne will inevitably involve decisions like this, and there is a case for a suitable public-sector oversight body, such as the ANAO, to observe in real time the unwinding of contracts and the treatment of confidential information.

Fourth, in providing services—such as policy advice, policy development and project-management service—that traditionally have been delivered by the public sector, the Big Four have become in some respects competitors to, and substitutes for, some functions of government. In Australia, the scale of the outsourcing of services to the Big Four is very large, and there have been calls during the PwC scandal to return those services to the public sector. The suggestion has even been made that the federal government should 'nationalise' the public-sector-related functions of one or more Big Four firms. (There have been similar calls in the United Kingdom.)

The Big Four compete with government departments and other government agencies in other ways as well. They are engaged in a competition for influence. Ministers and senior officials have looked to major consulting firms in the past as an alternative source of informal counsel.

The substitutability of Big Four activities for certain public-sector functions is a further complication. It is also a potential source of conflicting interests, such as when the firms might recommend in an advisory report that public functions should be outsourced.

Fifth, as well as standing alongside public-sector clients as trusted advisers, the Big Four sometimes sit on the opposite side of the table, advising corporates and other entities in conflict with government and, sometimes, in conflict with the public interest. Take, for example, tax avoidance or advice to cigarette manufacturers and other heavily regulated industries. The Big Four dominate the global tax-avoidance industry, with their services estimated to cost taxpayers more than US$1 trillion per year in lost revenue.

The firms have had their share of tax scandals. In 2005, the US Department of Justice accused KPMG of marketing tax shelters that were 'abusive' and 'fraudulent'. In 2013, a British parliamentary committee report described the tax authorities as fighting an unwinnable battle against the Big Four's provision of sophisticated avoidance advice.

Sixth, in numerous ways, the Big Four are sources of integrity risk for governments and public-sector agencies. Risks arise from political donations and the recruitment of former ministers and senior officials into senior Big Four roles. Problems with 'revolving door' personnel movements between government and the Big Four have previously been identified in the United Kingdom and Europe, and the issue also has been prominent in the PwC scandal in Australia. There also have been calls for an end to Big Four political donations—PwC Australia has already pledged it will no longer make donations to any political parties.

And finally, a role for the Big Four that is somewhat more abstract than the others and more pervasive: weaver of the neoliberal ether. During the peak decades of neoliberalism, the Big Four have been champions and extenders of that pattern. Their consulting toolkit, along with their general advice and advocacy, has helped perpetuate neoliberal ideas and expand the scope of their application, such as into social services and environmental policy. Standard neoliberal tools in the Big Four kit include asset-valuation methods, 'cost of capital' concepts, risk-management tools, project-management tools and market-based instruments, all of which have helped neoliberal ideas maintain a dominant position in public policy—even though several of the tools rest on fragile or contentious theoretical and empirical foundations.

To borrow a term from finance, the Big Four have been able to arbitrage across and between their respective service lines. The phenomenon of arbitrage involves exploiting differences across separate markets, such as by buying an asset in one market and selling it for a premium in another. The Big Four have engaged in reputational and branding arbitrage between auditing, advisory and tax services. Auditing gives their brands an aura of integrity, and the firms have exploited that aura in other, non-audit fields.

They have also engaged in informational arbitrage across their different relationships with government, such as between their relationships as advisers and their relationships as competitors and counterparties. In the United Kingdom and elsewhere, the firms have seconded consultants to tax authorities, to provide advice on tax law changes. The consultants have advised corporate clients on the same changes. Such relationships have been described as 'poacher, turned gamekeeper, turned poacher again'.

Through this arbitrage strategy, the Big Four have successfully monetised gaps in public-sector regulation and oversight of their conduct. The benefits from reputational and informational arbitrage seem to be significant drivers of the firms' overall diversification strategy.

With the Big Four having grown large and profitable by walking both sides of the street in their relationships with governments, conflicts of interest loom large. Ian Gow and Stuart Kells's 2018 book *The Big Four* warned that, by 2023 or thereabouts, the regulatory, technological, cultural and commercial tensions facing the Big Four would necessitate radical changes in how they were structured and how they operated. Today, the tensions have predictably intensified, and the firms are more or less on schedule.

The firms' diversified, multidimensional arbitrage strategy is no longer viable. One reason for this is that there exists a new culture of institutional openness, and there are new technologies enabling that culture. A wave of transparency has swept through hitherto dark places such as navy ships, locker rooms, casting couches and the offices of tax advisers. Arms-length commercial functions that depend on secrecy are increasingly untenable.

The diversified model has an impending use-by date for other reasons, too. Governments and regulators around the world have increased their scrutiny of the Big Four. A natural next step will be to require the firms to unwind their highly diversified mega-partnerships.

The identified conflicts of interest in Australia have escalated to become an existential moment for the Australian PwC partnership. In recent years, regulators have baulked at the idea of the Big Four turning into the Big Three or fewer. Those scenarios, regulators feared, would have systemic consequences for corporate governance and potentially for the financial system and the wider economy.

Those fears were misplaced. All of the Big Four service lines have substitutes, and indeed, most of them are subject to significant competitive pressure, including from innovations such as AI and 'audit bots'. The Big Four have successfully positioned themselves as seemingly indispensable, but in reality they are certainly not 'too big to fail'.

Stuart Kells is Adjunct Professor at La Trobe University's College of Arts, Social Sciences and Commerce, and Honorary Senior Fellow in Federation University's Collaborative Research Centre in Australian History. He has published numerous books and shorter works.

THE POWERFUL FIRMS THAT PUT THE 'CON' INTO CONSULTING

James Guthrie, Macquarie University; Jane Andrew, University of Sydney; and Erin Twyford, University of Wollongong

Daily revelations in the media surrounding the performance and bad behaviour of the consulting industry highlight a growing scandal that threatens more than just the firms involved. Attention so far has focused chiefly on PwC, which is not only embroiled in an ugly tax scandal, revealing serious conflicts of interest, but has been linked to the notorious Robodebt scheme. PwC failed to provide a seventy-page report to the government on this scheme, which was later ruled to be illegal, despite being paid nearly $1 million. Instead, it compiled an eight-page PowerPoint presentation.

Emerging evidence suggests these transparency failures and issues of conflict of interest at PwC are just the tip of the iceberg for the consulting industry.[9] KPMG has been accused of submitting inflated invoices and billing the Department of Defence for hours never worked, and EY was working for gas giant Santos while advising the NSW Government on new gas developments. Pressure is mounting on the consulting firms, particularly due to a Senate inquiry shining light on a system in which these firms are allowed to police their own behaviour.

Such is the apparent disdain some of the international firms hold for transparency and accountability in the Australian arms of their businesses that Boston Consulting Group (BCG), commissioned for more than $64 million since 2021, has rejected the opportunity to appear at the Senate inquiry. McKinsey & Company, which has 650 employees in Australia and signed up to an estimated $56.4 million worth of government work over the past two years, will apparently take the same approach. This repeats a 2021 inquiry into Australia Post, during which the pair refused to front the politicians.

A key issue is that governments worldwide, including Australia's, rely heavily on consultants. In 2021, the global consulting services market was valued between US$700 billion and US$900 billion. This universal reliance on consulting firms is highlighted in Mariana Mazzucato and Rosie Collington's 2023 book *The Big Con: How the Consulting Industry Weakens Our Businesses, Infantilises Our Governments, and Warps Our Economies*, which explains how consulting firms are structured to maximise returns to partners. It means the firms regularly engage in unethical behaviour, which continues to go unchecked in the absence of regulation.

In our submission to the Senate inquiry into consulting services based on our work as critical accounting academics, we mentioned the case of Bain & Company, a Boston-based global management consulting firm, which illustrates state capture by the consulting industry. State capture refers to cases where private interests influence a state to seek private advantage. The British Government banned Bain from tendering for government contracts for three years because of 'grave professional misconduct' in South Africa. Subsequently, during Jacob Zuma's two-term presidency, the South African Treasury banned the consultancy from tendering for government contracts for ten years. As a result, there is growing pressure on private-sector companies to remove Bain from their database of suppliers.

Similarly, McKinsey agreed to pay US$573 million to American authorities as part of a settlement for its role in the opioid crisis, which has killed hundreds of thousands of Americans.[10] The action was taken against McKinsey because of its conflict of interest in failing to disclose to the US Government's medicine regulatory body, the Food and Drug Administration, its work with Purdue Pharma, manufacturer of the synthetic opioid OxyContin. McKinsey continued to advise Purdue after the pharmaceutical company pleaded guilty to charges in

2007 that it misled regulators over the risks of the drug, leading to Purdue's bankruptcy a decade later.

These examples indicate the potential for action against consulting firms if the appropriate mechanisms exist.

Various Australian governments spend billions of dollars of taxpayers' money yearly on external contractors and consultants.[11] The NSW Government spent $1 billion on consultants between 2017 and 2022. Australia's top consulting firms secured a record $2 billion worth of Commonwealth taxpayer-funded work in 2021–22, with Accenture taking top billing for the second consecutive year. Australia's leading players offering consulting services include the 'Big Three' consultants Accenture (formerly Arthur Andersen), McKinsey and BCG, and the Big Four accounting firms: PwC, Deloitte, KPMG and EY. Despite this enormous expenditure, there is no transparency about what is provided and the knowledge these consulting services produce. Disclosure of perceived or actual conflicts of interest is limited to self-reporting and self-regulation.

Currently in Australia, three parliamentary inquiries are delving into the consulting industry and its relationship with the Commonwealth Government. The first, a Parliamentary Joint Committee on Corporations and Financial Services Inquiry, has heard allegations of, and responses to, misconduct in the Australian operations of the significant accounting, audit and consultancy firms (including but not exclusive to the Big Four) via a detailed investigation and analysis of regulatory, technical and legal settings, and broader cultural factors. The second is a Senate Economics References Committee Inquiry into Australian Securities and Investments Commission investigation and enforcement effort. The third is a Senate, Finance and Public Administration References Committee inquiry into the management and assurance of integrity by consulting services.

In our submission to the third inquiry, we raised concerns about conflicts of interest, the culture of consulting services firms, and the apparent lack of transparency and accountability in regards to consulting arrangements. We highlighted that the consulting industry in Australia is an unregulated activity.[12] This is because the unique structure of these consulting firms as partnerships means that regulation is focused on the individual via their membership in a professional accountant body or as a registered auditor or tax agent. This form of regulation is self-regulation in terms of codes and ethical practices.

There are few enforcement measures for integrity breaches and unethical behaviour by consultants and firms. Professional bodies, such as the accounting professional associations, take limited action on the misdemeanours of their members who are partners at Big Four consulting firms. Instead, information about the failures of transparency, conflicts of interest and unethical behaviour at these firms has resulted from the actions of various whistleblowers and investigative journalists.

This information has revealed that, despite their significant revenue, the Big Four firms are secretive partnerships, not companies, and do not have to disclose where their money is coming from, even though they are among the most powerful private institutions in the world. Most of their income growth comes from governments and large multinationals in work that does not even attempt to avoid conflicts of interest. Besides consulting, the Big Four also help multinationals minimise tax while simultaneously acting as 'gatekeepers' in auditing the same big companies. The dominant role played by the Big Four in transnational corporations' accounting and auditing practices is a global issue of concern, not just a problem for Australia.

PwC's Australian tax scandal was initially limited to one partner until PwC was forced to admit that multiple senior partners were involved after a cache of internal emails was released by a parliamentary committee at the start of May 2023.[13] The emails showed that PwC's embattled Australian affiliate misused confidential government tax information for commercial gain, creating a crisis that threatens to extend beyond national borders. This behaviour by individuals is consistent with a broad culture of conflict of interest, given that PwC provided advice to Treasury about international tax shifting while at the same time advising clients how to sidestep these laws.

When the 2015 *Final Report on the Base Erosion and Profit Shifting (BEPS) Action Plan* by the Organisation for Economic Co-Operation and Development (OECD) to tax transnationals was adopted in Australia in 2016,[14] PwC was already devising tax practices to sidestep the new law. The treasurer at the time, Joe Hockey, was concerned about the rise of opaque structures such as the 'double Irish, Dutch sandwich' that involved sending profits through one Irish company, then to a Dutch company and back to another Irish company in a tax haven. Such schemes were particularly popular with US tech firms, including Google (which has said it no longer uses the loophole). PwC tax partner Peter Collins signed confidentiality agreements with the Australian Government and fed intelligence on the government plans to PwC personnel in Australia and abroad. The firm used that information to give more than a dozen US companies an early warning of the changes, netting additional fees and potentially depriving Australia of tax revenue.

It has since been revealed in Senate Estimates that the ATO became aware in 2016 that a handful of multinationals 'suspiciously and quickly' sought to restructure operations in response to new tax-avoidance rules. Specifically, the ATO was concerned by tax schemes marketed by PwC that threatened the country's tax take and suspected confidentiality breaches. Information was passed to the police but it did not initially result in a full investigation. Treasury has since referred the matter to the Australian Federal Police (AFP), citing new evidence. The ATO also formally referred the issue to the TPB in

2020, which led to Collins being deregistered for two years. The TPB passed on 144 pages of internal PwC emails to the Senate.

The question of which colleagues received Collins's communications and what they did with the information will become a central part of future inquiries. While the scandal is Australia-centric, PwC used its global network to profit from privileged information, drawing in other parts of one of the world's biggest professional services firms. Its admitted failings are now subject to a police investigation, and governments worldwide will be taking note amid a growing reliance on private consultants to formulate public policy and public services. There are now multiple investigations into the leak, including by the AFP, and PwC has been banned from winning further work from the federal and several state governments.

Given that, for decades, PwC has provided tax advice to transnational companies, including miner Rio Tinto, meat giant JBS, energy company Chevron and explosives maker Orica, the current investigations could extend into the United States, United Kingdom and Europe, partly because the emails show PwC's Australian partners have shared the secret government information with PwC partners globally. Consider a report published in 2020 by the Global Alliance for Tax Justice that outlines how corporate 'profit shifting', otherwise known as 'tax avoidance', cost countries US$427 billion in lost tax revenue in that year alone.[15]

Nowhere is this kind of behaviour more evident than in the global fossil fuel industry. ATO data for the eight years from 2013 to 2021 show nine companies, including ExxonMobil Australia, Chevron, Santos, Peabody Coal, Yancoal Australia and QGC Upstream (a subsidiary of Shell), paid zero corporate income tax over that period. Those nine, along with sixteen other energy and resource companies with significant financial interests in fossil fuels, disclosed revenue of about $1425 billion. They paid an average of less than 1 per cent income tax on that revenue.

A host of offshore tax havens also enables manipulations of the Australian tax system. Contrary to popular opinion, the four wealthy nations of the United States, the Netherlands, Luxembourg and the United Kingdom, and the British 'independent' territory of the Cayman Islands, are responsible for 47 per cent of global tax losses. These firms are housed outside of Australia, where tax on earnings from Australian Government receipts does not feed back into the Australian economy. For example, Accenture plc is an Irish-American professional services company based in Dublin, specialising in IT services and consulting. A Fortune Global 500 company, it reported revenues of US$61.6 billion in 2022.

With this behaviour, management consultants are enablers of the new public management movement in which governments adopt structures, techniques and processes from the private sector to deliver public services. Consultants translate what they consider to be appropriate practices to novel public-sector settings. The significance of the consulting industry as the shaper of a new public sector is widely acknowledged.

Given the positioning of new public management as a movement with private-sector management practices and the use of the private sector to deliver public services as its fundamental reference point, the arrival of management consultants in public services is not surprising. Mazzucato and Collington outline how the consulting industry reached the core of global economies and governments. The 'Big Con' is possible in today's economies because of the unique power that consultancies wield through extensive contracts and networks, and the illusion that they are objective sources of expertise and capacity. An entrenched relationship exists between the consulting industry, hollowed-out and risk-averse governments, and shareholder value–maximising firms. Mazzucato and Collington demonstrate that global economies' reliance on companies such as McKinsey, BCG, Bain, PwC, Deloitte, KPMG and EY stunts innovation, obfuscates corporate and political accountability, and impedes the collective mission of halting climate breakdown.

In Australia, at the Commonwealth Government level, there has been a failure to account for how the performance of consultants is measured publicly. As outlined in our evidence to the Senate inquiry, the Treasury considers all consultants responsible for their performance management. A change in June 2023 has meant that suppliers must notify federal public servants if their personnel have had adverse findings against them as part of a new 'notification of significant event clauses', including an update to procurement rules introduced by the Department of Finance. The revised regulations emphasise that public servants 'must consider … a potential supplier's relevant experience and performance history when assessing value for money'.

Still, this approach relies on consultants self-reporting their performance and is profoundly inadequate, especially given the track record of these firms. But what is the alternative?

Mazzucato and Collington highlight that the Big Con has not only made millions for consulting firms but has hollowed out the public service. They propose a new vision, for the civil service to rebuild capability in public-sector organisations. It is essential to recognise the government as creating rather than wasting value. This requires implementing learning and adaptive processes, empowering risk-taking within public-sector organisations, and evolving the narratives around the government's role in the economy.

Busting up the consulting firms is the only solution to these issues. For financial markets, the conflicts of interest are just as untenable between the tax and audit divisions as the auditors are there to sign off the accounts as 'true and fair', while the tax advisers are there to advise corporations on how to most aggressively avoid paying tax in Australia.

Policymakers and the media will play a crucial role in this transformation. With a combined effort, we can end the Big Con once and for all, and restore an independent public service to its rightful place at the centre of government.

James Guthrie is an Emeritus Professor in the Accounting and Corporate Governance Department at Macquarie University. Professor Jane Andrew CPA is a professor of accounting and head of school at the University of Sydney Business School, and co-editor-in-chief of Critical Perspectives on Accounting. Dr Erin Twyford CA is a Senior Lecturer at the University of Wollongong.

BREAKING UP THE BIG FOUR IS THE ONLY SOLUTION

Allan Fels, University of Melbourne; and James Guthrie, Macquarie University

The Australian Government has so far failed to deliver on legislation that would bring the most significant breakthrough to date in forcing stronger tax and transparency regulations on multinational corporations. Reports suggest that these global giants, along with their professional enablers, lobbied against the proposed new laws.[16]

This is at a time when the PwC scandal has dominated headlines, with repeated criticism of partnerships by the government and various Senate inquiries.

The head of big four consulting firm EY has criticised rival PwC over the firm's tax leaks scandal, saying the alarming and disappointing conduct has rightly triggered intense scrutiny of the whole sector. The PwC scandal, along with multiple international inquiries, reveals that the only solution to resolve conflicts of interest between auditors, accountants and consultants is to break up the Big Four and other businesses performing audits. The role played by other major, non-audit-based consultants, such as McKinsey, BCG, Bain and Accenture, also requires a total overhaul regarding how they work for, and with, the government.

The major global audit market has essentially halved through consolidation since the mid-1980s, when there were eight large international audit firms. In the wake of the Enron scandal, its auditor, Arthur Andersen, was charged with shredding documents relevant to the investigations into the energy company. The revelation decimated the company's books and it was wound up in 2002. Since then, the market has reduced to four global majors: Deloitte, PwC, EY and KPMG. Between them, these firms have almost complete ownership of the market for audits of major companies worldwide. They audit companies that account for about 95 per cent of the Australian share market, 97 per cent of the London market's Financial Times Stock Exchange index, and over 99 per cent of the companies in the US market's Standard and Poor's 500 share index.

In a recent Senate inquiry, Allan Fels provided evidence that audit plays a critical role in the economy and should not be unnecessarily compromised. The fact that the Big Four provide consultancy, advisory and other services threatens to compromise the performance of audits and this should be prohibited by legislation. Other ways of dealing with the conflict appear not to work. The PWC scandal demonstrates that the Big Four cannot be relied upon to regulate themselves. Nor can legislation be relied upon: it has loopholes and is challenging to apply and enforce even when regulators try (which does not seem to happen now).

There is an actual and perceived conflict of interest when a firm conducting audits also seeks to do consulting work, whether for itself or others. In a previous inquiry into the audit firms in 2019, James Guthrie stated that conflicts of interest seem to be inherent in providing independent auditing services and being paid for these services year in and year out by the firm being audited. It is best not to overlay these conflicts with another set of potential conflicts, which merely heightens the possibility that auditors will not provide timely independent audits. Guthrie's submission indicated there are significant complications, pitfalls, costs and inconveniences in the compromise measures sometimes proposed as an alternative, such as internal separation of the functions within one firm.

The conflicts can never be entirely resolved, and where they go closer to being eliminated (or looking as if they are nearly eliminated), the rules and arrangements are typically costly to operate, with considerable external oversight required to ensure compliance. A clean, clear and sensible solution is much more preferable. The early July 2023 spin-off of PwC's government services to private equity buyers for $1 leaves doubts about the effectiveness of the consultancy's purge and how the industry could be reshaped.

During the 2023 Finance and Public Administration References Committee inquiry into the management and assurance of integrity by consulting services, Guthrie highlighted that the work of consulting organisations was often found to be rife with conflicts of interest. Examples include advising leading fossil fuel polluters as the government mandated to reduce the level of national emissions, auditing a sizeable prime contractor while simultaneously bidding for similar contracts, and writing federal tax legislation while advising clients on how to minimise tax obligations.

Senators Deborah O'Neill and David Pocock have been the critical inquisitors during the Senate investigations of PwC, which resulted in a report titled *PwC: A Calculated Breach of Trust*. The report's introduction acknowledges 'the scale of significance and substantial public interest in the matter of PricewaterhouseCoopers' (PwC) conduct about Australia's anti-avoidance tax laws, dating back to 2013. Subsequent reports will deal with the broader range of matters arising from the inquiry's activities which extend to the more significant consulting industry.'[17]

The dominant role in accounting and auditing practices of transnational corporations played by the Big Four is a global issue of concern, not just a national problem. On 22 June 2023, the Parliamentary Joint Committee on Corporations and Financial Services resolved to inquire into the Australian Securities and Investments Commission's capacity and capability to respond to reports of alleged misconduct. A growing body of international research has clearly documented how transnationals and their legal and accounting advisers engineer the law and the various regulatory structures to their advantage. Elected officials routinely support legislation that advantages the interests of business and industry over the interests of the public. Business and industrial elites gain and maintain their influence over political and bureaucratic elites through lobbying, political donations and revolving-door appointments between government and industry.

As a matter of priority, the various parliamentary inquiries now underway should investigate conflicts of interest and dubious ethical practices by the Big Four and those legal firms that provide aggressive taxation advice.

These entities enable companies to refashion themselves as 'transnational' and avoid paying taxes on revenue earned in national jurisdictions. Such inquiries should review the social licence and social contract of the individuals and entities that provide such aggressive taxation advice. Action could then be taken to withdraw such licences and contracts from those individuals and entities engaged in unethical and tax-avoidance practices.

Our principal recommendation is that the Big Four accounting partnerships in Australia use a structural split, rather than an operational split, in the audit and consulting parts of the firm. Under this, audit firms would do audit only, and neither the firms nor their associates would be permitted to sell any consultancy to audit clients. If the Australian Parliament legislates for a structural split of the Big Four, it would go some way to addressing the current problems, and hand the ability to rebuild its institutions back to the Australian public sector.

Allan Fels AO is an Australian economist, lawyer and public servant, most widely known in his role as chairman of the Australian Competition & Consumer Commission (ACCC) from its inception in 1995 until 30 June 2003. James Guthrie AM is an Emeritus Professor in the Accounting and Corporate Governance Department at Macquarie University, and joint editor of the interdisciplinary accounting journal Accounting, Auditing and Accountability.

BREAKING THE BILLION-DOLLAR ADDICTION TO CONSULTANTS IN GOVERNMENT

Denis Saint-Martin, Université de Montréal; and
Chris Hurl, Concordia University

The revelation that the Canadian Government spent C$15 billion (U$11.2 billion) on consultant contracts in the 2021–22 fiscal year dogged Prime Minister Justin Trudeau's administration all through 2023. It cast new light on the 2019 appointment of former McKinsey global managing director Dominic Barton as Canada's ambassador to China—McKinsey received around C$100 million (US$74.9 million) worth of contracts in 2021–22. The appointment, queried at the time, was scrutinised in a 2023 investigation into the large sums flowing from government coffers into private consultancy firms.

During Barton's tenure at the helm of McKinsey, the company pitched a pharmaceutical company on aggressively marketing OxyContin and other highly addictive opioids to Canadians. In a leaked memo published in *The Globe and Mail*, McKinsey told Purdue Pharma it could help determine whether there were opportunities to 'better target and reach high-potential prescribers', and help motivate the company's sales representatives to 'better align the sales force goals to company objectives'. The following year, Barton was a pro-bono economic adviser to the newly elected Trudeau. In fact, under Trudeau, costs for consultancy services have 'ballooned', with some estimates reporting a US$5.25 billion increase in spending between 2015 and 2022. In June 2023, a government review of federal contracts with McKinsey found 'no evidence of political interference', but it acknowledged there were 'always opportunities to further improve and strengthen' the government's contract-procurement process.

Companies like McKinsey are for the most part privately owned by the partners who run them. They are accountable only to themselves. The products they sell are theories, concepts and methods. The services they provide are intangible, the effects unknown and difficult to measure. This makes it difficult for governments and large corporations to assess whether they are getting their money's worth when using consultants.

Governments calling on consultants for advice on strategy and organisation is not a new phenomenon in Canada. As far back as 1918, the Unionist coalition in power in Ottawa was criticised for its use of 'pseudo experts' from the Chicago firm Arthur Young (which later became EY) in its reform of the public service. Today, consultancy firms have become the keepers of secrets for the world's biggest companies and most powerful governments. As advisers and confidants, firms have become the private repositories of top decision-making knowledge across a wide range of areas and organisations in business, society and the public sector. It has served them well. Sources vary, as firms are not required to report on their revenues, but the global management consulting market in 2022 was estimated at nearly US$700 billion.

Pre-COVID-19, the policy influence of firms like McKinsey, KPMG, Deloitte and Accenture tended to be exercised behind closed doors, and only when the issues were seen as technical concerns; that is, not politically salient. The pandemic changed everything. 'Privatised policymaking' suddenly became more visible to the public. In many countries, the high costs of using consultants became politically noisy, with governments and consulting firms feeling the backlash.

McKinsey was not only subject to an inquiry in Canada but also was embroiled in a 2022 investigation in France into suspected tax fraud. EY received a two-year ban on some audits in Germany in April 2023 over a scandal involving insolvent payment processor Wirecard. Scandals have also followed Deloitte and Bain in South Africa and PwC in Australia.

In the United Kingdom, a top minister argued Whitehall had been 'infantilised' by consultants. In 2021, a plan to limit the government's reliance on external consultants through an in-house 'Crown Consultancy' was announced, then dropped in 2023 before it ever materialised. In 2022, the UK Government reportedly awarded £2.6 billion (US$3.3 billion) worth of consulting contracts, a 75 per cent increase since 2019.

French President Emmanuel Macron's government was found by a Senate committee investigation to have signed contracts worth at least US$2.4 billion with consultancies since 2018. It also found many examples of 'revolving doors' between McKinsey consultants and the president's inner circle.

There remains debate over exactly how much influence consultants hold over governments, and it varies from country to country, but consultants are involved in all stages of policymaking. Some believe consultants are brought in to provide specialist technical skills or to rubber-stamp decisions already made by political elites. Others argue that consultants have effectively colonised the public sector, raising concerns about policymaking at large being privatised—potentially granting private interests more dominion over government than the public. But there's little credible evidence to suggest consultants have become shadow governments, pulling the strings. Instead, attention has shifted to the ties that bind consultancy firms to governments and companies.

Consultancy services are in a state of change. The management consulting industry is expected to bring in US$860.3 billion in revenue in 2023. Most consulting revenue comes from manufacturing and consumer products, financial services, and media, tech and telecommunications, but a growing share is also coming from government (10.5 per cent in 2022) and government-adjacent services, such as energy and utilities (10 per cent in 2022) and health services (10 per cent in 2022). The market for consultants runs wide, from huge transnational professional service firms (Deloitte, KPMG, PwC, EY) and strategy consultancies (McKinsey, BCG, Bain) to small niche enterprises run by sole operators.

The remarkable growth of management consultancy in the public sector has generated extensive debate in academia about why demand has increased. Ask a different discipline and you'll hear a different theory. Functionalist and economic theories may say policymakers often use management consultants because of their efficiency in addressing the complex tasks and technological problems faced by modern governments. Consultants provide a wide variety of highly specialised technical skills that would be more expensive to produce inside the civil service. Sociologists, meanwhile, may view consultants not as efficiency experts but as knowledge brokers between business and government. They are agents of legitimation who help transfer practices and principles into organisations that make them seem more rational and efficient. Consultants define the norms and disseminate models of appropriate action in the management of large organisations.

In these explanations, the growing demand for consultants' services in government comes from pressures to make public organisations more business-like. Or, as political theorists may say, it's about power relations. In one version of political theory, public-sector demand for consultants grew sharply with the election of neoliberal leaders who sought to bypass the blockages and inertia of public administration and break the monopoly of the civil service over policy. In another, it started with the expanding consulting profession and industry, and its ability to shape clients' demand for its services. According to this perspective, consultants are the sources of 'demand inflation'. They themselves influence the decision to hire outside experts by creating uncertainty while also offering a readily available solution. They make clients addicted to, or over-reliant on, their expertise.

This, in part, speaks to the changing source of power of these firms. Beyond relying on consultants themselves, consulting firms are also increasingly providing the platforms that governments rely on in order to operate, giving them infrastructural power. As the COVID-19 pandemic revealed, governments all over the world depend on the global database and analytics provided by the world's biggest firms to coordinate their responses to crises.

The growing infrastructural power of these firms has been reflected historically in their shifting organisational form. British public services expert Antonio E Weiss has observed at least five different 'waves' of consulting. The first began in the late-nineteenth century with the ascendancy of cost accountants and efficiency engineers, such as FW Taylor, who set out to rationalise the labour process under the guise of scientific management. It was followed in the 1950s and 1960s by the rise of accounting firms, promising organisational restructuring for large companies, and strategy firms, who offered to show the public and private sectors how they measured up against one another. By the 1970s, these services had been eclipsed with the rise of IT consultants, who set out to computerise administrative services. Finally, from the 1990s onwards, outsourcing firms entered the fray, promising to go beyond consulting on infrastructural IT rollouts and actively participate in the day-to-day administration of public services, blurring the line between advising on public services and directly delivering them.

As management experts Matthias Kipping and Ian Kirkpatrick noted in 2013, these different kinds of consultancies did not replace one another. Rather, they've been integrated into overlapping forms of service delivery, with many firms offering a multitude of services.[18] And while the field is quite diverse, there are indications that the industry has become increasingly concentrated over the past four decades. From the 1980s onwards, transnational professional service firms have grown their market share, often cross-subsidising consulting services and gaining entry through other services, such as accounting. Firms have been able to heavily invest in new technologies, taking advantage of their scale and scope in order to generate network effects. The industry is expected to continue consolidating, forging larger, globally connected companies, as well as complex partnerships bringing multiple consultancies together under single contracts.

Consultants can be convenient lightning rods and scapegoats. But the more governments delegate to consultants, the more consultants acquire intimate knowledge of a

LACHLAN GUSELLI & ANDREW JASPAN

government's internal operations. This insider knowledge is an asset for private consulting firms and can result in information advantages, causing various dependencies and rent-seeking behaviour by consultants. It makes the optics of, for instance, Trudeau's appointment of Barton as the Canadian ambassador to China seem problematic, even though no wrongdoing has come to light.

Critics of this new normal use the term 'consultocracy' to describe the 'increased power of consultants over politics, public governance, and public sector practices'.[19] Their work suggests that short-term, outsourced expert knowledge production is increasingly replacing the long-term work of civil servants and diminishing public agencies' policy capacity. The time has come to better regulate the consultocracy, exercising better control over the revolving doors between government and consultancy firms. Consulting firms should be subject to stricter disclosure requirements and codes of conduct.

And, while the firms are reined in, the analytical and research capacities of the civil service should be boosted. It serves the public interest to have a civil service that can attract the best talent and compete with the big consulting firms.

Denis Saint-Martin is Full Professor in the Department of Political Science at Université de Montréal. Chris Hurl is Associate Professor in the Department of Sociology and Anthropology at Concordia University.

CONSULTING FOR COVID: OUTSOURCED EXPERTS OR OVERPAID TEMPS?

Andrew Sturdy, University of Bristol Business School

Consultancy.UK, one of the leading voices in the industry, spoke in March 2020 of a darkening outlook: 'UK consulting market books slowest growth in seven years.'[20] With Brexit weighing heavily on the local economy, the numbers predicted a wider global downturn. The NHS, which a month earlier had claimed parts of it were 'seriously financially unstable', was meanwhile dealing with the sixth death from the spreading COVID-19 virus, which would be announced as a pandemic the next day by the World Health Organization. By the end of the month, 1789 people would be dead from the virus, while the prime minister, health minister and future king had tested positive and the entire country was in lockdown.

It wasn't only the NHS that was struggling. The functions of government within the United Kingdom were already working overtime to keep up with the pace of a nation undergoing enormous change stemming from Brexit. Taxpayer money spent on consultants within the government had been increasing year on year, from £700 million in 2016 to £1.2 billion in 2019–20. These numbers would surge during the pandemic, with the UK Government spending £2.5 billion in 2020–21.

The media was full of stories about how much governments were spending on consultants to support various pandemic-related activities, a cost which might have been justified on the basis of the scarcity of expertise and the short-term nature of the role. By October 2020, it was reported that £175 million had been spent, with *The Guardian* claiming: 'The government has bought consulting services from almost 90 different companies as it scrambled to fill gaps in the civil service's pandemic response.'[21] By the end of the pandemic's first full financial year, government and public bodies had issued £664 million in COVID-19 consulting contracts.

However, no-one seemed to be questioning why management consulting firms would have the requisite skills to organise for a pandemic—or, at least, why they would have better skills than, say, civil servants, healthcare managers, or even regular and cheaper temporary staff such as interim managers. Indeed, in the absence of any convincing case for specialist skills, it seems that consulting firms were used as expensive 'temps'. By 2022, the UK Government had reportedly contracted £2.8 billion worth of work from consultants, while the NHS quadrupled its budget on outside advice in the same year. Spending caps brought in more than a decade ago by then British prime minister David Cameron appear to have been quietly dropped within the halls of power, despite the constant reaching for the consultant's button being described as a 'lazy habit' by Cabinet minister Theodore Agnew.

So, what else could the government do to deal with a pandemic? The concept of a government department solely set up for such rare events, brought into action when required, staffed by experts, and deploying the latest technologies, might seem ridiculous. Nevertheless, some sort of contingency or capacity, perhaps shared by multiple governments, is more plausible. However, in the United Kingdom and elsewhere, there was no such availability. Because, as many claim, the public sector has been 'hollowed out' to the extent that when extra staff are needed, there is no capacity.

This is the dominant view in most research and news media, with the added irony that public-sector staff cuts are often the result of earlier advice from the consultants issued the contract to analyse the efficiency of government departments. However, this does not explain why the most expensive option is chosen, and for a sustained period. Research suggests that the strong brand (for some) of management consulting in general, and specific firms in particular, is important. This reflects deference to private-sector 'solutions' over civil/public service expertise and values, as well as close and 'revolving' relationships between decision-makers and consultants. In short, senior civil servants and politicians have developed a consulting 'habit'.

In fact, this is sometimes the case whether or not their own management is hollowed out. The use of external consultants is higher where there are more managers—consultants are not simply substitutes. And it is difficult, if not impossible, to establish whether others would have done better than externals for less. A further irony is that the immediate availability of consultants was partly founded on a COVID-induced downturn in consulting business generally, which should have led to a significant reduction in rates.

If it is true that governments have been hollowed out, the obvious question should be: what can be done to fix it? What lessons can be learned from the COVID experience, and what, if anything, has changed? For example, a new 'crisis' is being constructed by consulting firms around AI, which will be leveraged to sell more business.

First, however, we should note that many of these issues are not new, even if the scale of government consultancy use has extended beyond the early neoliberal adopters. This means that various policy options are readily available, and some are even in use and occasionally relaunched. Watchdogs such as national audit bodies and parliamentary accounts committees have repeatedly urged government departments to plan for future demand for generic skills (for example, project management) and, in the case of new specialisms, to insist on knowledge transfer and sharing from consultants as a priority.

A recent example of this is the publication by the UK Cabinet Office of a *Consultancy Playbook*, which is used to help clients and purchasing departments become more effective. Similarly, in 2022, The Australia Institute called for the publication of consulting reports to government departments. Such initiatives conform to demand-side approaches more generally which prioritise various forms of insourcing such as internal consulting and, when this is not possible, professional purchasing.

These need to be implemented more effectively, but also reinforced. For example, they could be combined in the idea of public–public (not private) partnerships that trade skills between similar agencies, or 'progressive purchasing', which is more specific and flexible. Likewise, 'scrial purchasing' could be introduced, where repeat business with a particular supplier is highly constrained. More could be done with systems to share not just knowledge gained from consulting projects but also evaluations of firms' or individuals' performances—something akin to an internal Tripadvisor or ratemyconsultancy.com. The latter illustrates the idea of governance through the market, an approach which, in general, would find favour among some clients and consultants.

The problem—one that plagues many policy issues in consulting—is that management consulting is mostly ambiguous, opaque and often co-produced with clients. This can make it hard to specify in advance and identify clear failure or poor quality, or attribute blame for it. Clients need to rely on trust and may well also not want their own actions made transparent. This is one reason why many are not keen on a more transactional or transparent approach to purchasing and may seek to resist or bypass rules. The classic example is 'chaining', where a large number of small projects are created to avoid invoking the need to make a business case, which is required for projects over a certain size. Reputation concerns are a clear impediment to transparency.

For these and other reasons—such as the reluctance of politicians to invest in internal resources for the long term—demand-side governance is vulnerable. In the United Kingdom, for example, the 2023 removal of a fees cap on government departments noted earlier and the closure of a government-wide internal consulting alternative suggest that the political will to govern consultancy usage is intermittent at best. Besides, there will always be some need for external advice. Perhaps additional attention could be given to the supply side. Here, governance, beyond that which applies to any service and the market, has been difficult or has taken the form of self-regulation. This comprises mainly professional ethics codes for which there is little evidence of enforcement or prospect of improved effectiveness.

Where most attention is needed is in the reform of the reward systems in consulting which prioritise 'sell-on'—the selling of further or repeat business, regardless of client need, to secure long-term income and short-term rewards. This applies to both global firms and individual practitioners as well as those in-between. It partly derives from the importance of trust, noted above, which makes securing new versus repeat clients a costly and time-consuming business. However, it is also rooted in the structures of large firms where selling, not effectiveness, is the key criterion for promotion and financial reward—'eat what you kill'. The traditional partnership structure was long considered to temper individual greed by sharing profits among partners, but this also encourages long-term tenure of senior managers who therefore seek long-term business growth. Such structural reform, along with the need for firms to declare to their clients any conflicts of interest—for example, other clients—is the most pressing policy issue.

Even with the introduction of more balanced 'scorecard' reward systems and demand-side pressures such as serial purchasing, broader organisational structural change is required. This implies a shift in values as well, perhaps towards those of traditional professional notions of being 'social trustees'. In particular, external consulting operations, where selling and profit are not the driving forces of business or even of the (management) services offered, could be developed further. Historically, these are quite common, such as bodies linked to industry associations or organisation development and process-based consulting traditions

There are also signs that alternative approaches are appearing and in demand. With the financial and climate crises, combined with technological developments and the values of gen Z recruits, new forms of consulting seem to be emerging that have a different ethos or structure.

One example is the B Corp (benefit corporation) model of purpose-led business that makes companies accountable to stakeholders, not just to shareholders or other owners such as partners. However, such an approach might sometimes be more of an exercise in branding or 'cosmethics' than different values or priorities—a de-growth consulting firm has yet to be found!

At the same time, even if consultants can be considered to be 'genuinely radical' or progressive, as Soline Blanchard suggests in her work,[22] it is important to acknowledge that the paid consultant role is ultimately to serve clients; that is, 'servants of power'. And, as Jeremy Fyke and Patrice Buzzanell write in their work on consultants selling 'conscious capitalism', clients are often very conservative and so they limit the possibility for change.[23]

Nevertheless, compared to the relentless neoliberalism that has held sway since the 1990s, there is at least some potential here for such new forms of consultancy to do more than simply exploit a hollowed-out and sometimes addicted civil service via 'expensive temps'. And, in our emerging post-COVID world, it would certainly be more effective in the long term than a permanent department for pandemics.

Andrew Sturdy is a Professor of Organisation and Management at the University of Bristol.

STRIKING THE 'RIGHT BALANCE' KEY TO SOLVING CONSULTANCY CONUNDRUM

Andrew Podger, Australian National University

There was a time when Australia's public service essentially ran the national government's functions on its own. In the 1970s, the APS had a workforce of over 250 000. There were nowhere near as many managers as there are today and, while university degrees were rare, the technical skill set was far broader. Fifty years later, the service is very different. The workforce is 40 per cent smaller despite Australia's population almost doubling, the proportion of senior positions has increased dramatically, and a new graduate workforce has replaced the former ranks of people with different technical skills.

Much of the transformation has been driven by technological change, but policies towards the public service have also changed dramatically. To keep the country running today, governments rely on external contractors, consultants and labour hire, with billions of taxpayer dollars being spent. However, serious questions are emerging about the value for money involved, with a series of scandals arising about the performance of contractors and consultants and how they won contracts.

The time is ripe for rebalancing, for giving back to the public service some of the control it has had taken away.

The APS today compared to fifty years ago is much smaller, much more top-heavy, more inclusive, particularly in terms of gender, but far less diverse in its skill sets and the functions it performs. 'Externalisation' is one of three major themes in public service developments from the 1980s in Anglophone countries, along with 'politicisation' and 'managerialism'. In Australia, early signs of some of these themes emerged with the Coombs royal commission of 1976 and its motifs of increased responsiveness to the elected government; greater efficiency, effectiveness and representativeness; and more open interaction with the Australian public.

The first big step came with the commercialisation of Australia Post and Telecom initiated by the Whitlam government and implemented under the Fraser government. Almost half (45 per cent) of the APS had been employed in the Postmaster-General's Department (PMG) and were then made employees of the new statutory corporations. The first stages of new public management in the 1980s focused on better 'management for results', with the managerialist agenda including a form of program budgeting based on clear program objectives and performance targets, and devolution of management authority subject to accountability for performance.

Gradually, these reforms embraced competition as managers, looking to improve efficiency and performance, began to test markets for various corporate services. Centralised administrative services such as property, construction and cars were turned into businesses and subject to competition. Defence commercialised its aircraft and ship building and maintenance businesses, along with munitions and clothing manufacturing, and then began its commercial services program of reform to reduce the costs of support services such as equipment maintenance, supply depots and canteens. Most departments explored the contracting out of various corporate services such as payroll.

In the wake of the Council of Australian Governments' National Competition Policy in the early 1990s, a wider range of utilities and services were subject to competition and, increasingly, the option of privatisation was pursued. The Commonwealth Employment Service was replaced by a program of services purchased by the Employment Department and delivered by for-profit and not-for-profit providers. Competitive tenders focused on achieving specified employment outcomes. Until then, the Australian approach towards new public management could best be described as pragmatic rather than ideological, with each incremental development focused on improving efficiency and effectiveness. Legitimate questions can be raised about the assumptions involved and the improvements achieved, but the agenda was being promoted by senior bureaucrats as much as by political leaders.

Ideology began to play a more explicit part from the late 1990s, though much of the agenda was still focused on genuine efficiency gains. Ideology was apparent, for example, in the mandating of IT contracting in the late 1990s, rather than allowing managers to determine when and where contracting offered efficiency gains. A *Yellow Pages* approach was also suggested, where any activities that private businesses revealed in the *Yellow Pages* that they delivered were not to be undertaken by government itself but instead outsourced. The imposition of staff ceilings in 2014, in addition to budget caps on administrative expenses, also forced some agencies to contract out activities even when there was no value-for-money advantage.

By this time, governments of both stripes had also become attracted to the apparent (political) advantages of external consultants, including both the appearance of a greater degree of independence of government and the public service, and the reality of close control to deliver acceptable advice. The 'politicisation' agenda was also downgrading the importance of strategic policy advice from the public service and giving priority to external policy advice, including through ministerial advisers and consultants subject to their close influence.

Data on the scale of externalisation in these earlier periods are not readily available, but the reduction in full-time APS employees reveals the dramatic impact of the commercialisation of PMG in the mid-1970s and suggests another significant impact over the 1990s. While APS employment grew over the following decade, that growth was in line with overall population and employment increases in Australia. There subsequently has been a further decline in APS employment, particularly relative to total employment.

The Audit of Employment conducted by the Finance Department and APS Commission in 2023 estimated that external labour paid for by APS departments and agencies in 2021–22 amounted to 53 911 (full-time equivalent, or FTE), compared to the actual APS staffing of 144 271 (average staffing level). Fifty-two per cent of these were outsourced service providers (mostly involved with Defence), 33.7 per cent were contractors, 12.5 per cent were labour hire and 1.8 per cent consultants. IT and digital solutions was the job family with the largest expenditure, representing 32 per cent of the external FTE and 43 per cent of the expenditure.

This does not reveal the growth in external labour. It is likely that Defence, which has 76 per cent of the total external labour, has always used external labour in its capital procurement and, since the mid-1990s, has also done so in its supply activities. Other departments are unlikely to have used much external labour until the 1990s.

There is some data on the increased use of consultants. The ANAO reported in early 2023 that the value of consultancy-related contracts increased from around $350 million in 2012–13 to nearly $900 million in 2021–22.[24] It appears the definitions may have changed, as in its 2020 report, the ANAO referred to growth from under $400 million to over $1.2 billion in the decade to

2018–19. A separate empirical analysis found spending on consultants in 2017 was 5.5 times that in 1995–96.[25]

There is evidence of improvements in efficiency over the early reform period, and there remains political and bureaucratic support to maintain the broad management framework that allows externalisation where it adds value. Serious questions have emerged, however, about the scale and management of externalisation and its impact on public service capability. Among these is whether the APS has retained sufficient capability to be an informed purchaser of external support, with the risk of not obtaining value for money even where external support may be warranted.

More recently, a series of reports and reviews has found that both politicisation and externalisation have gone too far. The APS of the early 1970s was too independent and too insular, and it needed to be more responsive to the elected government, more open in its dealings with the public, and more exposed to competitive pressures and external expertise and views. But the scale of increased political control and use of external labour over the last three decades has adversely affected the capability and performance of the APS, and led to some other fallings.

The impact on APS capability has been revealed in the Moran report, subsequent capability reviews, the Thodey report and a 2021 Senate inquiry. Areas of concern that were identified include strategic policy advising; human resources management; financial, performance and risk management; digital capacity; and APS capability as an institution. Important recommendations have been made to address both politicisation and externalisation concerns, the latter including the removal of staffing caps; reduced reliance on external consultants, contractors and labour hire; the development of 'professions streams', including in digital, data and human resources expertise; improvements in 'commissioning' external support; and better reporting on external labour.

The use of long-term contractors sitting beside APS employees doing similar, ongoing work (which it seems is not unusual) also raises a fundamental constitutional issue. If they are in effect Commonwealth employees, they should be employed under powers authorised by the parliament, such as the *Public Service Act*. That might also make them subject to legislated codes of conduct.

So, what to do?

The Morrison government endorsed the development of professions streams and established a Finance Department centre of excellence on procurement, referring to this in responding to the Thodey recommendation for improved commissioning. But it rejected the other Thodey recommendations to remove public service staffing caps and reduce the reliance on external consultants, contractors and labour hire.

The Albanese government moved swiftly to remove the staffing caps and, in its first two budgets, to reduce expenditure on external hires. It also commissioned the Audit of Employment as an important step towards better reporting on external labour. The use of labour hire and contractors has been reduced over the past year, but it will take time for the APS to rebuild capability so that it can fully take up the slack.

The replacement of labour hire by APS employees, including non-ongoing employees, should not present a major challenge, and it should ensure better trained and better motivated staff in service-delivery areas such as Services Australia and Veterans Affairs. Replacing highly skilled contractors, however, will require the APS to develop appropriate classification and remuneration arrangements that attract, develop and retain the skills required. Contracting for particular services may still offer value for money, but a cadre of internal experts is critical to identify when that is appropriate and to manage the process well.

Revelations through the current Senate committee inquiry suggest there also remain serious issues about the way consultants are used and the management of conflicts of interest.[26] Among the disciplines needed when contracting consultants are:

- clarity about what is to be delivered
- a competitive process

- careful management of the consultancy to maximise the quality of the product and manage any conflicts of interest
- proper assessment of the product against the description in the requirement
- where possible, publication of the material delivered to ensure it is exposed to external scrutiny.

While there is no doubt that the use of external labour has gone too far, it would certainly be wrong to suggest that we should wind back the clock to a world when the APS ran everything itself without the use of external organisations and labour. The challenge is to get the balance right.

The APS needs to retain a wide range of specialist skills, complementing generalist administrative and policy analysis skills. It needs those specialist skills to perform its very wide range of functions, and to have the expertise to be an informed purchaser when it does draw on external support. And there is more work to be done to ensure that its procurement processes are properly managed.

Andrew Podger is an Honorary Professor of Public Policy at the Australian National University and was a long-serving public servant.

CONSULTANTS FIND CLIMATE CRISIS IS GOOD FOR BUSINESS

Christopher Wright, University of Sydney

The global climate emergency is proving very lucrative for consulting firms. As the preferred advisers to governments and the world's largest corporations, management consultancies have discovered that designing policies and shaping the regulation of climate responses is a new and very profitable line of business.

One of the best recent examples came in Australia in April 2021, when then prime minister Scott Morrison hastily announced his government's long-awaited modelling outlining a pathway to net zero by 2050. Stressing a heavy emphasis on carbon offsets, new technologies and limited reduction in fossil fuel extraction, the modelling had been prepared not by the government's major scientific body, the Commonwealth, Scientific and Industrial Research Organisation, but by the world's most expensive and elite management consulting firm: McKinsey.

Despite costing the Australian taxpayer over $6 million, the modelling, as critics quickly noted, contained dubious assumptions, ignored the cost of future climate impacts, and notably failed to outline how net-zero carbon emissions would actually be achieved by mid-century.[27] Nevertheless, the choice of McKinsey as the expert modelling these scenarios seemed to fit with a government keen to continue the expansion of the fossil fuel sector. McKinsey, after all, had worked for forty-three of the 100 largest carbon polluters in the world.

It wasn't always like this. In Australia, as the political 'climate wars' raged during the 2010s, and prime ministers rose and fell on the back of various climate policies, many large corporations were already anticipating the regulatory, reputational, market and physical risks that climate change would inevitably bring to bear on their operations, and were establishing sustainability functions in response. Yet, throughout this period, the management consulting industry, which prided itself on being at the forefront of predicting future business risks and opportunities, seemed remarkably quiet on an issue which scientists and policy analysts had long recognised posed an existential threat to the future of our societies—and, indeed, a large proportion of life on the planet.

Sure, on the back of the Stern review in the United Kingdom in 2006, McKinsey had developed a greenhouse gas–abatement cost curve that had been promoted in different countries, and boutique sustainability consultancies had emerged to work with corporate clients on report writing. However, climate change, and environmental sustainability more generally, was seen as something of a niche area for management consultants, and certainly not a core driver of consulting revenue.

If there was a point when this changed, it was when Mark Carney, as head of the Bank of England, gave a speech at insurance giant Lloyd's of London in 2015 in which he highlighted the threat climate change posed for stranded carbon assets.[28] Soon afterwards, the Financial Stability Board published recommendations for the disclosure of climate risk in corporate financial reporting, and major institutional investors like BlackRock, HSBC and the Norwegian Sovereign Wealth Fund announced plans to reduce their exposure to fossil fuel stocks and focus on 'green' investment opportunities. Climate change had suddenly arrived in the halls of finance and the major consulting firms began to pay attention.

While management consultancies like to present themselves as management fashion-setters, research suggests that, if anything, they tend to follow the demand preferences of their corporate and government clients.[29] Since the 2015 UN Paris Climate Agreement, in which 195 of the world's governments committed to take action to avoid warming the planet more than 1.5 degrees Celsius above pre-industrial levels, the key question has been how that might actually be achieved. While the traditional policies of emissions regulation through carbon pricing and taxes have been seen as too politically contentious, in the intervening years the policy answer has been for government and, increasingly, large corporations to commit to achieving net-zero carbon emissions by mid-century. Here, then, has been a ready source of demand for advice into which the world's large consulting firms have now entered.

What started as a trickle of sustainability consulting suddenly transformed into a flood and, in the past few years, management consulting has found its climate mojo. The Big Four accounting majors quickly snapped up smaller boutique sustainability consultancies to establish their own climate and sustainability practices, and bullishly announced multibillion-dollar investments in environmental, social and governance capabilities.

In 2021, BCG established its own Center for Climate and Sustainability, and the firm was announced as the 'Consultancy Partner' for the twenty-sixth Conference of the Parties of the United Nations Framework Convention on Climate Change in Glasgow (COP26). Not to be outdone, shortly afterwards, the most venerable of the blue-chip consulting firms, McKinsey, launched its own new practice, McKinsey Sustainability, and its regular publications were now filled with advice and reports on the urgency of climate change and how different industries could seize the opportunities of the new climate economy.

However, as evangelists for the neoliberal economic order, global management consultancies face a dilemma in advising governments about how to tackle the climate crisis. Any meaningful response to global warming actually requires the rapid cessation of fossil fuel energy use and an industrial-scale shift to renewable energy sources—no mean feat in a world still reliant for over 80 per cent of its energy needs on coal, oil and gas. Moreover, any consulting advice to governments or business needs to square with the clients' commitment to continued economic growth and the maximisation of shareholder value, while at the same time giving some appearance of future emissions mitigation. Not surprisingly, much of the net-zero policy advice falls on the net side of the equation, with a heavy emphasis on carbon offsets (paying others to plant forests, or at least promise not to cut forests down), the expansion of costly technologies of carbon capture and storage, and investment in as-yet-unproven carbon removal via direct air capture.

Missing here is the inconvenient truth that the world's carbon budget to avoid dangerous climate change has now run out, and that even the International Energy Agency now argues there can be no new oil, coal or gas development if the world is to have any hope of achieving net-zero emissions by 2050. Yet, a perusal of *McKinsey Quarterly*, or indeed any of the other major consultancy publications, reveals a surprisingly upbeat story for the fossil fuel sector in the short to medium term. Yes, there will be a decline in coal as an energy source, but oil and gas are still seen as stable investments over the next decade. There's also a rosy future ahead for renewables, as well as hydrogen, bio-feedstocks and carbon capture and storage. As an elite government and corporate adviser, it pays not to talk down potential future clients and markets.

Many of the big consulting assignments are not just in the corporate sector but, increasingly, working for governments. This shift to public-sector consulting has a long history, with major consultancies like McKinsey, BCG and Accenture having provided advice and implemented changes in public-sector settings such as health, education, social services and utilities for many decades. As the philosophy of new public management has spread around the world, so the 'politicised expertise' of management consultancies has been used by governments to justify the neoliberal retreat of the state from the provision of public services. It has also led to some disastrous policy outcomes, such as McKinsey's work in advising governments in developing economies on the REDD+ program aimed at reducing rainforest deforestation, which paradoxically resulted in policies increasing deforestation.[30]

A major problem in advising governments, and the public sector more generally, is that, unlike the established public service bureaucracy, which at least in the Westminster system maintains a level of independence and the ability to provide advice to government 'without fear or favour', management consultancies are profit-seeking commercial businesses. Their survival depends upon winning and maintaining client relationships such that an ongoing line of business contracts is maintained.

As critics have noted, the large consultancies work across multiple industries and from project to project. Despite claiming they internally manage potential conflicts of interest through systems of 'Chinese walls', numerous corporate scandals from Enron to those of more recent times show these conflicts appear a feature of the business. Indeed, when it comes to climate change, it's not as if the consulting firms' own employees haven't noted the ethical and moral dilemmas of advising on emissions reduction while at the same time maintaining very profitable relationships with the key producers of the climate crisis. Some years ago, when researchers interviewed a partner in one large consultancy that worked for major coalmining companies, he noted that many of his younger consultants were quite passionate about climate change and did research in their own time, then added: 'That's nice, but if a client doesn't want to hear it, they're not allowed to say it!'[31]

While these tensions are often hidden from public view, in 2021, in the lead-up to COP26 in Glasgow, 1000 of McKinsey's own employees signed an open letter expressing outrage at the firm's continued engagement with the likes of BP, ExxonMobil, Gazprom and Saudi Aramco.[32] The signatories observed that the 'climate crisis is the defining issue of our generation'. They urged McKinsey to publicly disclose the aggregate amount of carbon pollution produced by its clients and warned: 'Our positive impact in other realms will mean nothing if we do not act as our clients alter the Earth irrevocably.' While the company's partners responded by claiming McKinsey should be seen as helping the planet transition to a net-zero future, its staff pointed out that much of the consultancy's work actually focuses on improving the efficiency of fossil fuel extraction and enhancing corporate profitability.

In the words of one departing employee: 'Having looked at the actual hours billed to the world's largest polluters, it is very hard to argue today that McKinsey is the "greatest private-sector catalyst for decarbonisation" … It may well be the exact opposite.'

Management consulting is an industry that has evolved historically in tandem with the emergence of industrial capitalism and management as a professional class. Far from the image it likes to portray as a provider of independent expertise and advice, consultancy is itself a global business driven by the profit motive and the need to maintain ongoing commercial relationships with its corporate clients. The fact that governments worldwide now turn to management consultants rather than their own public servants as the preferred source of policy and technical advice is an indicator of how thoroughly neo-liberalism has denuded and corrupted the state and the collective interests of civil society.

Climate change is now the most urgent and threatening issue facing the future of human society. It says something about the parlous state of our democratic institutions that, even on an issue of such critical importance, this, too, is now being handed over to the partisan whims of an already all-powerful corporate class.

Christopher Wright is Professor of Organisational Studies at the University of Sydney Business School and a key researcher at the Sydney Environment Institute.

UNIVERSITIES CAN HELP FIX GOVERNMENTS HOOKED ON CONSULTANTS

Duncan Ivison, University of Sydney

The sheer scale of the use of consultants and external contractors in Australia's levels of government is staggering. According to the Centre for Public Integrity, the use of 'management advisory services' by the Australian Government went up by 1276 per cent over the past decade.[33] The overuse of these external contractors has been headline news in Australia for much of 2023. The breaches of confidentiality and conflicts of interest that have been exposed have rightly been the subject of public outcry. There is a feeling, too, that these advisers are used to rubber-stamp or legitimise policies public servants are no longer capable of developing themselves, either because they lack the capacity to do so or are afraid to.

While it's reasonable for the government to call on external experts for help dealing with the myriad complex issues facing the country, there are downsides, as the PwC scandal has shown. Consultants have little incentive to offer genuinely impartial and frank advice, given the commercial incentive to maintain their client relationships. As a result, we get bad policymaking and the hollowing out of state capacity, and the public good loses out.

Whether or not the consultancy industry is mainly to blame for this hollowing out, there is no question that we need now, more than ever, a more active, creative and capable public service, given the scale and urgency of the challenges Australia and the world face. It's no wonder that people are increasingly exasperated by government inertia and partisan bickering while—quite literally—the world burns.

One way to address this is to think more boldly about the way we harness expertise across the public and private sectors to address the challenges we face. If we could close the gap between the groundbreaking research carried out in universities and institutes, and the ability of policy-makers and industry to use those insights to address our collective challenges, perhaps we'd be better off as a nation.

Right now, one in four people working for the public service is employed externally rather than directly by government, through a combination of consultants, contractors, labour hire and outsourced service pro-viders. This amounted to over $600 million in 2021–22 of taxpayers' money in contracts with the Big Four consultancies, with a further $1 billion for future work. Prime Minister Anthony Albanese's Labor government is moving to reduce this expenditure and the reliance on external firms. But the current debate gives us a chance to ask some deeper questions about what else might be happening. Why have governments, along with other public institutions, including universities, come to rely on consultants so heavily?

The more cynical explanation is that the big consul-tancy firms will often recruit former senior civil servants to work for them. Those recruits bring their networks and inside knowledge to the business and build trust with their government clients, who are often former colleagues. Senior civil servants like outside firms because they provide independence from government and thus greater flexibility regarding the advice they provide. The recent royal commission into Robodebt shed light on the dark side of this process. Advice that is politically uncomfortable can be quietly buried and projects wound up in ways that would be more difficult if they were being carried out within the public service itself.

However, we shouldn't allow cynicism to overwhelm our analysis. For one thing, there is no question that specialised expertise is sometimes required from outside of government to address highly complex issues. It's not surprising that governments have turned to consultants for help in relation to defence and IT, for example, given the limited scope of expertise within the public service in these areas. It's also understandable that extra help can be required for critical projects to deliver them on time.

Much of the criticism of governments' overreliance on consultants has focused on the cost, blatant breaches of confidentiality, and conflicts of interest. This reinforces a general sense that managerial elites can take advantage of their position to pay themselves first, usually at the taxpayer's expense. But an overreliance on commercial firms to provide expertise also undermines the public service precisely when governments face increasing demands from the public to address deep societal and global challenges. This is by far the biggest issue emerging from the debate about the role of consultancy firms that we should be focusing on.

Banning consultants or external contractors in government isn't practical or desirable since there are times where they are genuinely needed. Tougher guidelines about managing conflicts of interest, and more investment in boosting the capabilities of the public service (starting with the funds that were being spent on consultants), are critical. However, we also have an opportunity to think more deeply about how we can draw on expertise from across society to improve public debate and decision-making given the challenges we face.

Mariana Mazzucato and Rosie Collington's book *The Big Con* captures an important aspect of this conundrum. The gist is that state capacity for responding to the problems our societies face today has been weakened since the neoliberal reforms of the 1980s and 1990s, introduced and sustained by all sides of politics, which limited government to focusing mainly on market failures. The role of government has thus become essentially reactive—'enabling', 'fixing', 'de-risking' and 'redistributing', as opposed to intervening and investing directly to create new solutions. The view has been that real value is created by business and entrepreneurs, not governments.

But this approach has turned out to be doubly mistaken. First, governments can and do invest directly to help create value. Mazzucato's example from her previous book, *The Entrepreneurial State*, on how government-backed research helped build the iPhone, is a killer example of this, as is the role that publicly funded mRNA research played in the development of vaccines for COVID-19. However, it's also problematic because business doesn't invest in basic research. Moreover, at least in Australia, business is failing to adequately invest in research and development (R&D) more generally.

Mazzucato and Collington claim that the 'infantilisation' of governments has been aided and abetted by the way consultants are used. Governments and businesses use PwC, McKinsey and the like to provide expertise and validate policies. To make it worse, because the big consultancies' largest clients are sitting on both sides of the table, so to speak, they have little incentive to offer genuinely impartial and frank advice. The country loses out as a result.

To turn this around, reinvesting in our public service is crucial. But we also need to think more boldly about the way we harness the expertise in innovation, science, the social sciences and the humanities across the public and private sectors to address the issues we face. The key is how.

First, we could re-energise and reinvest in our R&D sector. Just about every study over the last decade in Australia and overseas has shown that investing in research delivers one of the best returns on investment governments can make.[34] However, in Australia, investment in R&D in both the public and private sectors is declining. Business expenditure on R&D fell from 1.37 per cent to 0.92 per cent of gross domestic product (GDP) between 2008 and 2019—well below the OECD average of 1.92 per cent. Government expenditure declined, too, from 0.33 per cent to 0.17 per cent of GDP between 2000 and 2020.

Meanwhile, universities have been picking up the slack, raising their investment in research from 0.40 per cent of GDP in 2000 to 0.61 per cent in 2020—taking their share of the nation's total spend on R&D to 37 per cent in 2020. Overall, we are spending 1.8 per cent of our GDP on R&D, well below many of our competitors and the OECD average of 2.7 per cent. Universities also do almost all of the basic research conducted in Australia, but which in turn is declining as a proportion of all research done. This is a worrying development at a time when we need new ideas to address our biggest policy challenges.

Fortunately, we have the opportunity through the government's Australian Universities Accord process to tackle some of these issues head-on. It's an opportunity we can't waste. But even if we can get the funding right, there is still more to do. We need new bridges and pathways between government and the R&D sector to help rebuild state policymaking capacity in areas such as climate, health and technology, among others. This means forging new kinds of partnerships between governments,

universities, research institutes, community organisations and industry. It also means a change in Australia's
research culture.

This means we need to continue to create policy
incentives for universities to think creatively about the
impact of their research. We can do this by encouraging
pathways for the commercialisation of research, to get it
out into the world more quickly. We can also encourage
community-engaged and community-led research, to
ensure we are not only aligning more of our research
with community needs, but also learning from close
engagement with the users of our research on the ground.
We also need universities to reward and value this work
within their internal incentive structures, including how
staff are assessed, remunerated and promoted.

Finally, we should be encouraging greater mobility
between academia and the public service. If the movement between the upper echelons of the civil service and
consultancy firms is currently something of a vicious
circle, then we need to create more-virtuous circles
between public good–oriented institutions like universities and research institutes and the public service (as well
as with industry). Australia is poor at doing this (with
some notable exceptions) compared to other countries
like the United States.

But we also need new kinds of institutions. A greater
diversity of universities and colleges with distinct
missions and areas of focus, rather than everyone being

incentivised to look the same, would help. Australia could use its own version of the London School of Economics and Political Science, for example, or a Caltech, or something like the Institute of Fiscal Studies, to help train future policymakers and inform complex policy debates. Again, the Universities Accord process offers us an opportunity to explore these possibilities.

We also need more of what are called 'bridging initiatives'. For example, in New South Wales, the University of Sydney, the University of Technology Sydney, and Western Sydney University joined forces with the state government to create a new public policy initiative, which this author helped lead. This was inspired, in part, by the government's desire to tap into the expertise held in NSW universities that could help them address their most difficult policy challenges. Hence, the James Martin Institute for Public Policy was born. It has a mandate to work closely with the public service in co-designing and collaborating on policy-related research, and orienting its work around the priorities the public service and government are grappling with. It also has a mandate to help researchers develop the skills required to produce policy-relevant research. It's off to a great start.

Of course, there are similar initiatives elsewhere in Australia, including the work done by the Crawford School of Public Policy at the Australian National University, the Melbourne School of Government, the Sydney Policy Lab, as well as private think tanks such as the Grattan Institute, the Centre for Public Integrity, the Australia Institute, and Blueprint Institute. We need more of these, and greater interaction between them and governments at the state and federal levels, to lift our capacity to develop public policy suitable for the complex times we live in.

Focusing on the harm that an overreliance on consultants can cause isn't enough. We need to rethink and reinvest in the intellectual infrastructure of our country to help our governments and policymakers make better decisions in all of our interests.

Professor Duncan Ivison is Professor of Political Philosophy in the Department of Philosophy and helps lead the James Martin Institute for Public Policy.

NOTES

1   Oxford Reference, 'Overview: Neoliberalism', 2023.

2   Maximilian Walsh, 'Lobotomising the Public Service', *The Bulletin*, 19 May 1981, p. 26.

3   Consultancy.com.au, 'PwC and Accenture the Lead Consultants for Covid-19 Vaccine Rollout', 24 January 2021, https://www.consultancy.com.au/news/2885/pwc-and-accenture-the-lead-consultants-for-covid-19-vaccine-rollout (viewed August 2023).

4   Julianne Schultz, 'How Morrison Killed the Public Service', *The Saturday Paper*, 12 February 2022, https://www.thesaturdaypaper.com.au/opinion/topic/2022/02/12/how-morrison-killed-the-public-service/164458440013316#hrd (viewed August 2023).

5   Jonathan Barrett, 'PwC Australia Scandal: What Actually Happened and Will It Be Fatal for the Advisory Firm', *The Guardian*, 1 June 2023, https://www.theguardian.com/australia-news/2023/may/31/pwc-australia-scandal-what-actually-happened-and-will-it-be-fatal-for-the-advisory-firm (viewed August 2023).

6   Special thanks to Reece Hooker, 360info Commissioning Editor, who assisted with the commissioning of the essays that follow.

7   RAW Rhodes, 'The Hollowing Out of the State: The Changing Nature of the Public Service in Britain', *The Political Quarterly*, vol. 65, no. 2, 1994, pp. 138–51.

8   Marty Bortz, We're All Managers Now: The Discursive
     Influence of Management Consultants, PhD thesis, University
     of Melbourne, 2019.

9   Colin Kruger and Rachel Clun, 'Why the PwC Scandal Is Tip of the
     Iceberg', *The Sydney Morning Herald*, 20 May 2023, https://www.
     smh.com.au/business/the-economy/why-the-pwc-scandal-is-tip-
     of-the-iceberg-20230517-p5d91p.html (viewed August 2023).

10   Michael Forsythe and Walt Bogdanich, 'McKinsey Settles for
     Nearly $600 Million over Role in Opioid Crisis', *The New York
     Times*, 5 November 2021, https://www.nytimes.com/2021/02/03/
     business/mckinsey-opioids-settlement.html (viewed August
     2023).

11   Ronald Mizen, 'Accenture Beats the Big Four in Record $2b
     for Canberra Work', *Financial Review*, 9 August 2022, https://
     www.afr.com/politics/federal/the-big-consulting-winners-from-
     record-government-spend-20220809-p5b8bb (viewed August
     2023).

12   Parliament of Australia, 'Parliamentary Business: Submissions',
     2023, https://www.aph.gov.au/Parliamentary_Business/
     Committees/Senate/Finance_and_Public_Administration/
     Consultingservices/Submissions (viewed August 2023).

13   Australian Treasury, 'Referral to the Australian Federal Police of
     the PwC–Collins Matter', media release, 24 May 2023, https://
     treasury.gov.au/media-release/referral-australian-federal-police-
     pwc-collins-matter (viewed August 2023).

14   Organisation for Economic Co-Operation and Development,
     'BEPS 2015 Final Reports', 2015, https://www.oecd.org/tax/
     beps-2015-final-reports.htm (viewed August 2023).

15   Global Alliance for Tax Justice, '$427 Billion Lost to Tax Havens
     Every Year', 20 November 2020, https://globaltaxjustice.org/
     news/427-billion-lost-to-tax-havens-every-year/ (viewed August
     2023).

16 Tom McIlroy, 'Labor Tax Plan Risked Global Transparency Efforts', *Financial Review*, 9 July 2023, https://www.afr.com/politics/federal/labor-tax-plan-risked-global-transparency-efforts-oecd-20230709-p5dmvy?btis (viewed August 2023).

17 Finance and Public Administration References Committee, *PwC: A Calculated Breach of Trust*, June 2023, https://parlinfo.aph.gov.au/parlInfo/download/committees/reportsen/RB000169/toc_pdf/PwCAcalculatedbreachoftrust.pdf (viewed August 2023).

18 Matthias Kipping and Ian Kirkpatrick, 'Alternative Pathways of Change in Professional Services Firms: The Case of Management Consulting', *Journal of Management Studies*, vol. 50, no. 5, 2013, pp. 777–807.

19 Matti Ylönen and Hanna Kuusela, 'Consultocracy and Its Discontents', *Governance*, vol. 32, no. 2, 2019, pp. 241–58.

20 Consultancy.UK, 'UK Consulting Market Books Slowest Growth in 7 Years', 10 March 2020, https://www.consultancy.uk/news/24001/uk-consulting-market-books-slowest-growth-in-7-years (viewed August 2023).

21 Jasper Jolly and Rajeev Syal, 'Government Spending on Covid Consultancy Contracts Rises to £175m', *The Guardian*, 16 October 2020, https://www.theguardian.com/politics/2020/oct/16/uk-government-spending-on-covid-consultancy-contracts-rises-to-pounds-175m-investigation (viewed August 2023).

22 Soline Blanchard, 'Feminism through the Market? A Study of Gender-Equality Consultants in France', *Gender, Work and Organization*, vol. 29, no. 2, 2022, pp. 443–65.

23 Jeremy Fyke and Patrice Buzzanell, 'The Ethics of Conscious Capitalism: Wicked Problems in Leading Change and Changing Leaders', College of Communication Faculty Research and Publications, https://epublications.marquette.edu/comm_fac/95/ (viewed August 2023).

24 Australian National Audit Office, *Australian Government Procurement Contract Reporting: 2022 Update*, report no. 11, 2023, https://www.anao.gov.au/sites/default/files/2023-02/Auditor-General_Report_2022-23_11.pdf (viewed August 2023).

25 Caspar van den Berg et al., *Policy Consultancy in Comparative Perspective: Patterns, Nuances and Implications of the Contractor State*, Cambridge University Press, 2019, https://research.rug.nl/en/publications/policy-consultancy-in-comparative-perspective-patterns-nuances-an (viewed August 2023).

26 Parliament of Australia, 'Senate Standing Committees on Finance and Public Administration', 2023, https://www.aph.gov.au/Parliamentary_Business/Committees/Senate/Finance_and_Public_Administration (viewed August 2023).

27 Graham Readfearn, '"Pure Spine": Experts Pan Coalition Net-Zero Modelling that Allows Gas Sector to Grow', *The Guardian*, 12 November 2021, https://www.theguardian.com/australia-news/2021/nov/12/pure-spin-experts-pan-coalition-net-zero-modelling-that-allows-gas-sector-to-grow (viewed August 2023).

28 Mark Carney, 'Breaking the Tragedy of the Horizon: Climate Change and Financial Stability', speech at Lloyd's of London, 29 September 2015, https://www.bankofengland.co.uk/-/media/boe/files/speech/2015/breaking-the-tragedy-of-the-horizon-climate-change-and-financial-stability.pdf (viewed August 2023).

29 Matthias Kipping, 'The Evolution of Management Consultancy: Its Origins and Global Development', in Barry Curnow and Jonathan Reuvid (eds), *The International Guide to Management Consultancy*, Kogan Page, London, 2003, pp. 21–32, http://ndl.ethernet.edu.et/bitstream/123456789/29689/2/78.%20Barry%20Curnow%20%2C%E2%80%8E%20Jonathan%20Reuvid.pdf#page=48 (viewed August 2023).

30 Greenpeace, 'McKinsey's "Bad Influence" over Rainforest Nations around the World', 7 April 2011, https://www.greenpeace.org/usa/news/mckinsey-rainforest-report (viewed August 2023).

31 Christopher Wright and Daniel Nyberg, 'Working with Passion: Emotionology, Corporate Environmentalism and Climate Change', *Human Relations*, vol. 65, no. 12, 2012, pp. 1561–87, https://journals.sagepub.com/doi/abs/10.1177/0018726712457698 (viewed August 2023).

32 Michael Forsythe and Walt Bogdanich, 'At McKinsey, Widespread Furor over Work with Planet's Biggest Polluters', *The New York Times*, 27 October 2021, https://www.nytimes.com/2021/10/27/business/mckinsey-climate-change.html (viewed August 2023).

33 Centre for Public Integrity, 'Opaque Big Four Contracts Increase 1276%', July 2023, https://publicintegrity.org.au/research_papers/big-four-contracts-increase-1276 (viewed August 2023).

34 London Economics, *The Economic Impact of Group of Eight Universities*, 2018, https://www.go8.edu.au/Go8_London-Economics-Report.pdf (viewed August 2023).